# MAKE NECKLACES

## 16 Projects for Creating Beautiful Necklaces

Quarry Books
Rockport, Massachusetts
Distributed by North Light Books
Cincinnati, Ohio

First published in the United States of America by:
Quarry Books, an imprint of Rockport Publishers, Inc.
146 Granite Street
Rockport, Massachusetts 01966-1299
Telephone: (508) 546-9590
Fax: (508) 546-7141

Distributed to the book trade and art trade
in the United States of America by:
North Light, an imprint of F & W Publications
1507 Dana Avenue
Cincinnati, Ohio 45207
Telephone: (800) 289-0963

Other Distribution by:
Rockport Publishers, Inc.
Rockport, Massachusetts 01966-1299

ISBN: 1-56496-271-7

10   9   8   7   6   5   4   3   2   1

Designer: Laura Herrmann Design

Printed in Hong Kong
by Regent Publishing Services Limited

# CONTENTS

# NECKLACE BASICS

Y OU DON'T HAVE TO BE A HIGHLY SKILLED PROFESSIONAL TO CREATE
beautiful necklaces that make you the envy of your friends. With just a little
imagination and the right materials and tools, you can produce wonderful works of art
from classic jewelry elements such as beads, precious metals, and stones. Or you can
transform mundane, household items such as buttons, fabric scraps,
and newspapers into sophisticated necklaces. To produce fabulous designs with a professional finish, you will need the
findings, tools, and techniques
that join, link, and make up
your necklace.

## Materials

Beads have been used in jewelry making since the beginning of time, but
they can be expensive to buy in large quantities. Many of the projects in this
book show you how to make your own beads using materials such as modeling clay and paper. The clays can be twisted together in different color
combinations to create wonderful marbled effects or built up into imitation
millefiori canes—a technique used more often by glass workers. Papier-
mâché beads can be painted to mimic ceramic beads or hand-decorated to
make them look extra special. Strips of colorful paper can be rolled to make
beads of different shapes and lengths. Pick up other materials at yard sales
and antique fairs. Never throw out a broken necklace—its remaining beads
and clasps can always be worked into other designs.

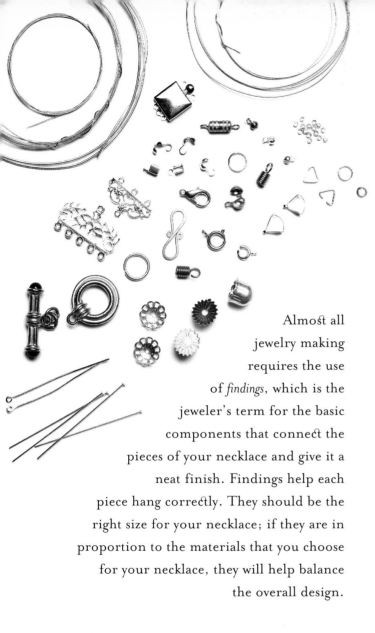

Almost all jewelry making requires the use of *findings*, which is the jeweler's term for the basic components that connect the pieces of your necklace and give it a neat finish. Findings help each piece hang correctly. They should be the right size for your necklace; if they are in proportion to the materials that you choose for your necklace, they will help balance the overall design.

# Findings

JUMP RINGS are circular or oval metal rings that are not completely joined together. They come in a variety of sizes and thicknesses to suit all kinds of jewelry projects. Use them to link two findings together.

CLASPS usually consist of two pieces, attached to each end of the necklace, that join together to secure it around your neck. They come in an assortment of designs, including the screw clasps, spring rings, barrel clasps, and S-clasps. You can also buy decorative two-part clasps that have preformed holes for more than one thread. These can be set with diamanté, pearls, or rhinestones. Choose a style that suits your necklace design.

HEAD PINS and EYE PINS are wire pins that come in various lengths to link beads to each other or to a necklace chain. A head pin, which has a flat head at one end like a blunt dressmaker's pin, is particularly useful for making pendant drops and charms. Eye pins have a preformed loop at one end and are most often used to link together beads or findings.

# Other Findings

Use JEWELER'S WIRE when head and eye pins are not long enough. It is available in gold and silver in many gauges and can be coiled into decorative spiral charms. The finer the gauge of wire, the easier it is to work with. Choose a wire thickness to suit the beads and the overall design of the necklace, especially if it is a visible part of the design.

CALOTTE CRIMPS conceal and secure knots at both ends of a necklace. They help make a finished necklace look polished. Calotte crimps come in different sizes to suit the thread you are using and in slightly different styles; round calottes can open sideways or from the top; square calottes are ideal for thicker threads and for clamping unusual materials such as feathers.

Other findings to use when making necklaces are ornate SPACERS and HANGERS, which often have two, three, or five preformed holes. End SPACER BARS can be used to make multistrand designs and to attach the clasp to the start and finish of a necklace. Incorporate more decorative spacer bars as part of the design itself. Large BELL CAPS are a decorative cap added to each end of a necklace to conceal a collection of knots. Join pendant clasps to jump rings to make a pendant or charm hang correctly, or directly clamp on to fabric or seed charms.

The most important findings are jump rings, calotte crimps, head or eye pins, jeweler's wire, and clasps. These may all sound rather strange now but by the time you have worked through the projects in this book, they will be much more familiar to you. All findings are readily available in craft stores, from bead suppliers, and even in department stores. You can buy them in precious or nonprecious metals. Buy plain findings to use for the less visible parts of a necklace; highly decorative findings work well for the more prominent areas on a necklace.

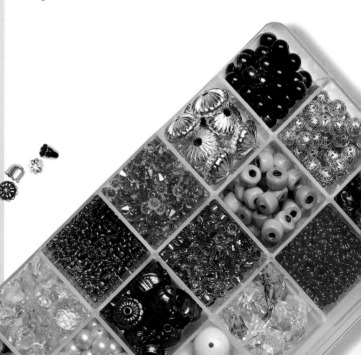

# Tools & Adhesives

All of the projects in this book are easy to make and require little space for their creation—most can be put together at the kitchen table with only the basic tools. Lay down a craft board to protect the table from damage, and provide a flat, even surface to work on. Organize your beads and findings in boxes and trays.

Small round-nosed and needle-nosed pliers, available at jewelry and bead suppliers, make opening, closing, and linking together findings much easier. Use round-nosed pliers to turn loops, and to twist and coil wire into shape. Squeeze calotte crimps together and flatten joints with needle-nosed pliers. Use two pairs of pliers to open and close jump rings. Buy them with integral wire cutters or invest in a separate pair of wire cutters for trimming head and eye pins, and jeweler's wire.

As a general rule, an all-purpose, clear-drying glue is all you will need to ensure that your wonderful design won't break when you wear it. Take the time to read and follow the directions on the glue container. Use common sense: make sure that bead and finding surfaces are clean and grease-free: and, with some glues, you may need to work in a well-ventilated room.

# Stringing & Knotting

Stringing beads onto thread is the simplest way to make a necklace. Before you begin, decide how long you want it to be. A long necklace should hang no lower than your waist or it will get in your way. A medium necklace is usually between 20 and 27 inches / 50 and 70 cm, and a choker between 14 and 18 inches / 36 and 46 cm. Add 3 inches / 7.5 cm on each side of the necklace to allow for knotting. To calculate the total number of beads you will need to make a necklace, count how many beads fit into 1 inch / 2.5 cm, then multiply this by the length required. The size and weight of the beads you choose determines which thread to use. Consider whether the thread will be visible, whether it will be strong enough to support the beads, and if it will fit through the holes in the beads. Silk and cotton thread both hang well and can be color-coordinated to the beads, but they are not very strong. Use several strands together if you are working with heavy beads. To prevent them from getting tangled, run them through a beeswax cake. Or try polyester thread already coated with beeswax. If you prefer the drape of the silk and cotton threads, knot between every bead or small group of beads to prevent the beads from tumbling in all directions if the thread breaks. A needle is helpful when you are drawing the knot up close to a bead. Make sure the knot is large enough to resist slipping through the bead hole.

When making a necklace with a central point of interest, thread both ends of the thread with a needle and work from the middle outward on both threads at the same time, keeping the design symmetrical. Another advantage of working from the center is that the length can be adjusted by adding or taking away beads at each end—you won't have to start all over again.

*To string a necklace with a central theme, work from the center of the necklace outward, to both ends of the thread.*

Fine, invisible thread, though not very strong, is useful for tiny lightweight beads like rocailles because it can be threaded through a beading needle. Nylon line and tiger tail are more substantial and will support most designs. They are both almost invisible to the eye and can be used without a needle. Nylon is inexpensive and easy to handle, but will not always hang well, so it is best for fun bead necklaces. Tiger tail is a good, all-purpose jeweler's thread. It is made from fine strands of steel cable in a plastic coating and is therefore very strong, but it does have a tendency to kink. It is easy to make

starter knots in tiger tail, though sometimes you need pliers to pull it tight, or you can make a loop and secure it with a crimp bead. Leather thong, decorative cord, string, and even raffia can also be used. Thong is good for stringing individual beads or small groups of beads or objects with large holes. String and raffia can be used to complement more unusual material, such as shells.

How you knot and finish your necklace depends on the length you choose. If it is long enough to go over your head, you can string on the beads and simply knot the two ends together. Add a blob of superglue to secure the knot and hide it inside a bead. For shorter necklaces, knot one end and secure in a calotte crimp (see *Findings*), string on the beads, and then knot and secure the other end to another calotte crimp. Calotte crimps have preformed loops that are easy to join to a necklace clasp with jump rings (see *Finishing Techniques*).

*Use a needle to knot right up to the edge of the bead.*

# Linking Beads

There are many other ways, besides using bead strands, to make necklaces. Link together groups of beads in similar colors with head or eye pins to form a necklace or to hang as charms. You can wire each bead individually, which is quite time-consuming but produces an expensive-looking finish, or work the beads in small groups. To make the beads go further and use up leftover beads, insert short lengths of chain between each group of beads.

To make charms, use a finding called a head pin, which is like a blunt, flexible sewing pin with a flat "head" at one end. They are cheap to buy, especially in large amounts from craft suppliers, and are particularly useful for making charms because the flat head prevents the beads from sliding off. If the head pin slips through the bead hole, add a small stopper bead first. Slide the beads onto the pin in the order you want, trim the wire with wire cutters if necessary, and then turn a loop with round-nosed pliers.

The loop can then be attached to a bead necklace with a jump ring or opened slightly and joined directly to a chain necklace.

Eye pins are ideal for linking beads together because they already have a preformed loop in one end. Use short pins for single beads and longer ones for groups of beads. Slide the beads onto each pin, trim the wire, and turn a loop, just as you would with a head pin. To link the beads together, use jump rings or open up a loop on the pin and join to the next loop. Make sure you close the loops securely or they will come undone when you wear them.

You can substitute jeweler's wire for the head and eye pins. To make charms, you will need to turn a small spiral in the end with round-nosed pliers. You can then leave this protruding as a decorative effect or turn it under so the bottom bead sits on it. For linking beads, simply turn a loop in each end with pliers.

# Multistrand Necklaces

To create more elaborate necklaces, work with multiple strands and add special clasps and other decorative findings to make the necklaces look polished. Multistrand necklaces can simply be several bead strands joined to one another or to an ornate spacer bar. More elaborate designs can be worked on more than one thread, split and worked individually, then brought back together.

To make the most basic multistrand necklace, bead lots of strands of similar lengths. Finish the ends with calotte crimps and link the loops of these together in a jump ring. The ends can then be disguised with a pretty bell cap (see *Finishing Techniques*). To use end spacer bars, select one with the same number of holes as the number of threads you are using—usually two, three, or five—finish each beaded strand with a calotte crimp, and join them directly or with jump rings to holes on the bar. You can also incorporate decorative spacer bars in the design, taking each thread through a hole as if it were a bead. Make sure you keep the threads in a straight line.

For a more sophisticated multistrand look, work on two or more threads, stringing beads onto all the threads for part of the design and individual threads at other points. With this style, it is important to work out your design first and to keep both sides of the necklace symmetrical. More textured effects can be achieved if you twist or braid the threads when they are worked on separately.

# Finishing Techniques

How you finish a necklace can make or break your design. To get a truly professional look, use

*Hold a jump ring with two pairs of pliers positioned at either side of the joint. Gently twist the ends away from each other sideways to open, and twist back again to close.*

findings—the tiny metal components used to link, join, and complete a design. Jump rings link together two or more pieces, such as a calotte crimp to a necklace clasp, or groups of beads and charms to a necklace, so they hang freely. To keep the shape of the ring, and to ensure that the two ends meet perfectly again, open the rings at the joint using pliers (two pairs of pliers are ideal), twisting the ends away from each other sideways rather than just pulling them apart. To close, simply twist the ends back again so that they meet exactly. Practice opening and closing them successfully.

End knots can look ugly and need to be disguised. For single-strand necklaces, a calotte crimp is usually sufficient; its preformed loop can be joined to a jump ring and necklace clasp.

*Place the knot at the end of a length of thread in the cup of a calotte crimp and squeeze the two halves together using needle-nosed pliers.*

position the knot in the "cup" of one half and use needle-nosed pliers to squeeze the two sides together. Make sure the thread is going in the right direction before you secure the crimp. If you are using calottes that open from the loop end, you will need to pass the thread through a small gap in the hinged end before knotting, then close in the same way as before. Use square calottes for

There are several calotte crimp designs to choose from. Round calottes look like tiny metal beads when they are closed. They are hinged either at the side or bottom and have a gap for the thread to pass through. For sideways-opening calottes,

*For this different style of calotte crimp, the thread is pushed through a hole in the base of the crimp before knotting. The two halves are then squeezed together.*

*These tiny crimp beads are used most often when working with tiger tail and are squeezed tightly with flat-nosed pliers to secure the loop in the tiger tail.*

thick cord or thong; they are open on one side, which is where you insert the thread. With needle-nosed pliers, fold one side over the thread and then the other side to secure. An alternative to calotte crimps, crimp beads, tiny metal beads, secure loops in the ends of nylon line or tiger tail. Simply thread them into position and squeeze firmly with pliers to secure.

Use calottes on multistrand necklaces when you are attaching a decorative end spacer, but if the design has lots of strands, add a bell cap to hide the calottes. This is a bell-shaped metal cap with a central hole. Slip the loops of the calottes onto a jump ring, but before closing the ring, push it through the loop of an eye pin. Insert the pin through the hole in the cap, trim it to about

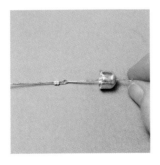

*A bell cap conceals a collection of knots or just adds a decorative end to a necklace. Slip the open eye of an eye pin through a calotte loop in the tiger tail. Close it securely. Push the pin through the central hole in the cap, and trim and turn a loop in the opposite end.*

⅜ inch / 1 cm with wire cutters and turn a loop with round-nosed pliers. Bell caps are often very ornate and come in a variety of sizes. Use the smaller ones as decorative ends on single-strand necklaces.

Once you have successfully concealed the knots, complete the necklace with a clasp. Choose a style to suit your design: screw clasps and spring rings are the simplest and most discreet in appearance. Two-part clasps are often more decorative (they can be patterned or set with pearls or diamanté), and they have more than one hole, which makes them ideal for multistrand necklaces. To attach a clasp to a neck-lace, open up a jump ring and slip it through the loop on the calotte and the hole in the necklace clasp, then close the ring. Two-part clasps have a corresponding catch, but for a spring-ring clasp, you will need to attach a jump ring to the other end of the necklace to complete the clasp.

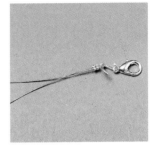

*A necklace clasp adds the perfect finishing touch to a necklace. To attach, simply insert an open jump ring through the loop at the end of the thread (or the loop of a calotte crimp) and through the loop on the clasp at the same time.*

# BEAD IDEAS

**A** VISIT TO YOUR LOCAL CRAFTS STORE WILL REVEAL AN array of beads to use in making your necklace. Or be adventurous and use objects you can find at home, such as pasta shapes or feathers from a feather duster, to substitute for beads. If you choose to make your own beads, try unusual materials, such as newspaper and magazine cuttings, colored foil, or fabric scraps.

## Clay Beads

One of the most effective materials to use is polymer clay. It is available in a fantastic range of colors, molds easily, and sets hard in a low-temperature oven. There are several comparable brands available, each with their own malleability, baking time, and color selection.

Plain beads in a single color can be molded into any shape you want and then decorated with acrylic paints (water-based paints don't cover as well). To make the beads, first knead the clay until it is soft and pliable, then roll it out into a log shape, ¼ to ¾ inch / .5 to 2 cm in diameter, depending on how big you want the bead to be. For tube beads, cut the log into equal lengths and pierce the center with a toothpick or knitting needle. Pierce the bead from both ends to get neat holes; if you just push the stick straight through, make sure that you smooth the rough edges where the stick emerges.

Round beads are made in the same way but each piece of clay is shaped into a ball in the palms of your hands. Pierce holes with a toothpick as above. Square beads are also made from a long log that is then flattened into a square against the edge of a knife or piece of wood. Cut to size and pierce as before. Add texture and detail to plain beads of any shape by pressing modeling tools, coins, and so on, against the surface, or by adding small strips or dots of other colors.

Experiment with several colors, for more exciting finishes, such as marbling or millefiori. To create a marbled effect, roll out logs of two or more colors and wrap them around each other. Knead these together, roll them back into a larger log, folding it in half and twisting until the colors are blended. Be careful not to knead too much or the individual colors will disappear and the clay will eventually return to a new, single color.

Shape beads as described above.

Millefiori or "thousand flower" beads, described in detail in *Magnificent Millefiori*, are slightly more complicated, but rewarding to make once you have mastered the techniques. Begin with a core color—either a plain log or two colors rolled together. Then place other logs in different colors around the core, completely surrounding it. The colors are usually placed in a regular pattern and must be gently pressed together to ensure no air is trapped inside. The whole cane is then wrapped in another sheet of clay, carefully rolled out to a diameter of about ¼ inch / .5 cm, and cut into tiny slices that are pressed on an unbaked base bead to cover it.

## Safety Note

Always read the instructions given on the polymer clay package. This clay gives off fumes, especially as it bakes, and should be used in a well-ventilated room.

# Paper Beads

Using paper is one of the easiest and cheapest ways to make beads. The simplest papier-mâché beads can be made by shaping pieces of newspaper into a ball and then layering pasted strips of newspaper over it. For a smoother finish, layer the paper strips over a ball of plasticine. When the ball is completely dry, cut it in half with a craft knife and remove the plasticine to lighten the paper beads. Glue the two halves of the bead back together and conceal the joint with another layer of paper before decorating. See *Pretty Papier-Mâché* for details on making papier-mâché beads.

To make rolled paper beads, use old wrapping paper or magazines, or paint your own designs onto plain paper; then cut into strips or elongated triangles, and roll up tightly around a toothpick. To give the finished beads a sheen and a durable finish, paint them with clear nail polish.

# Fabric Beads

You can use fabric to make all kinds of beads that can be decorated with embroidery or sewn stitches, or even with tiny beads. To make little puffs of fabric, cut the fabric out in circles, hem the edges, and draw up the edges. For tube beads, strips of fabric can be joined and gathered at either end. To give them shape, wrap them over a cardboard base or stuff with a little padding.

# Wooden Beads & Pressed Cotton Beads

Most craft suppliers stock unvarnished wooden beads and pressed cotton balls in a variety of sizes. These are both easy to paint and decorate in your own individual style. Support the beads on wooden skewers, tops of pencils, or old paintbrush handles while painting, and leave to dry on a knitting needle stuck in a block of plasticine or polystyrene. Keep patterns simple. If you want to use several colors, let each color dry before starting the next. When you are finished, protect the surface with a coat of clear varnish or nail polish.

# Miscellaneous Bead Ideas

Roll ordinary kitchen foil or colored candy foil wrappers to make bead shapes. Pierce the center with a sharp needle and thread into necklaces. Or add colored foil as a decorative final layer on a papier-mâché bead. Salt dough, which needs to bake in a low-temperature oven for several hours, is another good medium for making beads of different shapes. Both foil and clay can be painted and decorated to suit your design.

Pasta, seeds, nuts, and even washers can be painted, decorated, and strung into spectacular necklaces—no one will ever guess their origins. Use your imagination, and you will discover that all sorts of bits and pieces—safety pins, colorful paper clips, and even rubber bands can be turned into jewelry.

# CREATING A DESIGN

*Silver Crystal*
*Black — diamanté*

*Silver Spirals*

## Finding Inspiration

THE STARTING POINT IN ANY DESIGN IS FINDING INSPIRATION. IDEAS FOR jewelry designs can come from a visit to a museum or a library. Look to the ancient Egyptian, Roman, and Celtic civilizations, as well as the more recent Arts and Crafts and Art Deco periods, for ideas. A walk in the country or along the seashore can put you in touch with one of the greatest and most economical design source libraries: Mother Nature. Flowers and foliage, rocks and minerals, insect and animal life all can spur the imagination. The sky provides us with the sun, moon, and star motifs that are perfect for interpreting into jewelry forms. The sea washes up shells on the beach and sculpts pebbles and wood into interesting shapes.

Don't forget the materials you have on hand. Beads and fabrics can fall accidentally and often haphazardly together to create striking and unusual combinations. Paints and decorative finishes are fun to experiment with. Clays can be molded into unusual shapes and given textured finishes.

# Working Out a Design

Once you have found your inspiration, try to sketch out different ideas on paper. You will need a sketch book, tracing paper, pencils, colored crayons, felt tip markers (including gold and silver markers), an eraser, and a pencil sharpener. You don't have to draw works of art; rough sketches will suffice. Consider buying a special necklace tray that has channels for the beads to easily plan and make necklaces in two or three different lengths.

For simple necklace designs, start with a center point of interest, such as one of the beads you intend to use. Decide on the length you want (see *Stringing and Knotting*). Then sketch the sides, keeping them symmetrical—the necklace will look odd if one side is obviously different from the other. Take into consideration the length of your hair and the way you wear it; if it is long enough to hide the end of the necklace, you will not need to use special beads there.

As a general rule, most necklaces should be made from an uneven number of beads so that one will fall at the center. If you are adding a pendant or tassel decoration, however, use an even number of beads so that the pendant becomes the center point. To get the best visual balance with beads of different sizes, place the larger ones near the center and the smaller ones tapering off toward each end. The same principle also applies to any charms that you hang from the necklace.

After working out your basic design, pick the thread, clasp, and end fittings. To calculate how many beads you will need, count how many beads fit into 1 inch / 2.5 cm, then multiply this by the length required. Write down the findings you will need next to your design sketch. If you want to try any unusual paint effects or create complex millefiori beads, experiment with paints on paper before moving on to a sample bead.

# Long NECKLACES

$\mathcal{L}$ong necklaces are both beautiful and versatile. You can arrange them in double or triple strands, or simply let them hang long. Papier-mâché beads give the necklace texture and help keep long necklaces lightweight. Use polymer clays to create colorful beads that mimic real marble or Venetian glass (but are much less heavy), or to mold charms into stylized contemporary flower shapes. To create glamorous, retro designs, knot the strand midway for a 1920s flapper look. Or mix crystal and pearls to wear on a sparkling night out on the town.

Feel free to adapt the necklace designs that follow to suit your materials and needs. Try using jet black beads instead of pearls in the diamonds and pearls tassel necklace. Experiment with gold and colored stones for the Flowering Vine necklace. Use clays in strong jewel tones to transform the marbled beads into faux precious stones like lapis or malachite.

Pretty Papier-
MÂCHÉ

Sketch out your design on paper. Work out a color scheme, and the size and approximate number of beads you need.

Add an iridescent paint medium to the paint as you work or stipple on the finished beads to add luster.

Vary the shapes of the beads by altering the plasticine base—tubes, tear drops, and cubes are a few easy examples. When you get more experienced, experiment with hearts, stars, and even stylized animals.

Add hand-painted detail to each bead to add a decorative and more personal finish.

After you master the papier-mâché technique, use different types of paper to create unique finishes. Handmade papers, decorative foil papers, and even wrapping paper can be layered over the beads.

Take the time to give each bead two or three coats of varnish for a durable finish.

APIER-MÂCHÉ IS A CRAFT THAT HAS BEEN PRACTICED for centuries, so it's not surprising that it is enjoying a great revival. The techniques are simple to master; it uses everyday, inexpensive materials, and is remarkably versatile. The phrase "papier-mâché" actually means "mashed paper" in French and was first used by emigré workers in eighteenth-century London. Over the centuries, the techniques have been used to make an extraordinary variety of objects, including furniture, that prove to be as durable as they are beautiful. For the craft jeweler, it is a wonderfully adaptable modeling medium. This project uses one of the easiest papier-mâché techniques of layering pasted strips of torn paper over a base shape or mold. The beads are then painted in brilliant contrasting colors for a striking effect.

*Newspaper and wallpaper paste*

# PRETTY PAPIER-MÂCHÉ

## Getting Started

Mix the wallpaper paste following the instructions on the package. To make the beads, layer tiny newspaper strips, covered in paste, onto rolled plasticine balls. Cut nylon thread into a length of 30 inches / 76 cm plus 6 inches / 15 cm for knotting.

### PERFECT PAPIER-MÂCHÉ

Use torn strips of newspaper—the rough edges produce less obvious joints.

✦

Carefully overlap each piece and smooth edges with your fingers to release any trapped air or lumpy paste.

✦

Use two different-colored newspapers to make it easier to distinguish between the layers.

✦

You can use wallpaper paste or PVA glue as an adhesive. Wallpaper paste is easier to use as it's less tacky than PVA, but PVA produces a stronger finish. The two can be mixed together (to a consistency of thick cream) or use PVA for the last few layers.

✦

All the layers can be applied at once but the smoothest finish is achieved by allowing each layer to dry before applying the next.

## You Will Need

### FOR THE BEADS

Plasticine
Wallpaper paste
Paste brush
Torn newspaper strips
Craft knife
Thick sewing needle
PVA glue
Gesso
Paintbrush
Acrylic artist's paint
Varnish

✦

### FOR THE NECKLACE

Nylon thread
Calotte crimp
Needle
Small gold spacer beads
Necklace clasp

**1.** Roll the plasticine into balls the size you need. Remember that the finished beads will be a little larger with the added layers of paper.

**2.** Tear the newspaper into tiny strips and cover with wallpaper paste. Work on a ceramic or glass dish and paste several pieces of paper at the same time.

**3.** Carefully place the pasted newspaper strips all over the plasticine ball in a even layer, covering it completely. You will need about five or six layers to create a firm, finished bead. Leave to dry.

**4.** Place the hard ball on a cutting surface and use a craft knife to slice through the middle of the bead.

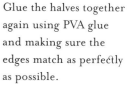

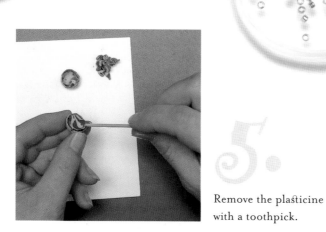

## 5.

Remove the plasticine with a toothpick.

## 6.

Glue the halves together again using PVA glue and making sure the edges match as perfectly as possible.

## 7.

Add another few layers of pasted paper to cover and smooth over the joint. Let dry thoroughly.

## 8.

Use a needle to pierce a central hole and insert a toothpick through the hole. Paint the beads with a gesso undercoat to cover the newsprint. Paint the beads in the colors of your choice. Let the bead dry on a toothpick in a slab of plasticine or in a piece of foam.

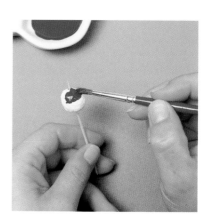

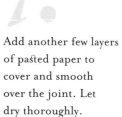

# Completing the Necklace

Tie a large knot in one end of the nylon and secure inside a calotte crimp. Thread the beads on in the order you decided. Then thread a small gold bead in between each papier-mâché bead. Knot the remaining end of nylon close to the last beads and secure in a calotte crimp. Use a jump ring to join the clasp to a calotte and add a jump ring to the other end.

## Variations on a Theme

Try painting the beads with graduated shades of green to add a more subtle dimension to the necklace (right).

For a striking effect, experiment with different shapes of beads painted in brilliant contrasting colors (far right).

This technique can be used to make a variety of charm shapes. Consult books on the history of jewelry or take a trip to a museum for inspiration.

Consider how the charms will link together when you plan your design.

Use scraps of clay to practice shaping your designs and bake to check how it will work. (If the clay is rolled out too finely, it will become weak and brittle.)

To wire the charms like beads, use a head or eye pin to make a hole, and leave in when baking to harden.

Choose a neutral-colored clay if you plan to use a painted finish.

For a jazzier look, make charms in lots of different colors.

SYNTHETIC POLYMER CLAYS ARE ONE OF THE MOST versatile of the newer modeling materials available for jewelry-making, and can, with a little creativity, be fashioned into expensive-looking designs. The soft and pliable clay makes it easy to mold or sculpt into almost any kind of shape you can think of, from basic beads to more intricate designs like these contemporary, stylized flowers. When hardened in a low-temperature oven and varnished or painted, the finished pieces can imitate precious metals or the finest porcelain but have the advantage of not shattering into little pieces if dropped. The clays are available in a wonderful range of colors that you can use as they are, or blend with other colors. The finished pieces also take on a totally different look when decorated with glittering jewel stones and metallic paint.

*Metallic paint, chain, and Fimo*

# FLOWERING VINE

## Getting Started

Break off a piece of Fimo and knead with your thumbs and fingers until soft and pliable. To join the flower charms to the chain, use jump rings large enough to fit over a petal of the flower, with room to move. Fimo varnish and silver powder mixed together can be applied to the flowers as an alternative to metallic paint.

## You Will Need

**1.**

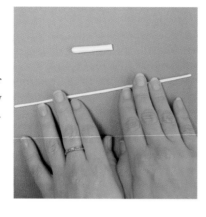

Roll out the Fimo after kneading into a very fine sausage shape.

**2.**

Make a small loop at one end.

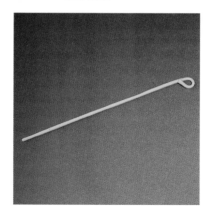

### FOR THE FLOWERS
Fimo in a neutral color
Metallic paint
Paintbrush
Tiny jewel stones
Strong craft glue
Varnish

### FOR THE NECKLACE
Chain
Pliers
Eye pins
Wire cutters
Crystal beads
Jump rings
Necklace clasp

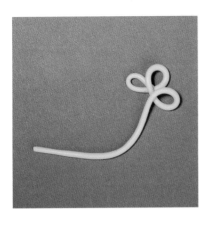

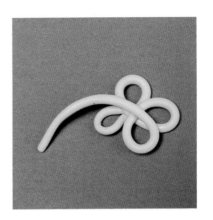

**3.** Lift up the other end of the sausage and make another loop at a 45° angle to the first, working counterclockwise, then make another loop in the same way so that it is a mirror image of the first.

**4.** Make the last loop to complete the shape and bring the Fimo to the center.

**5.** Cut off any excess at the center point and then very gently flatten the flower slightly with your palm.

**6.** Harden in a low-temperature oven following instructions for the Fimo. When cold, paint all the surfaces carefully with metallic paint. When dry, paint with varnish and leave for 24 hours before making into a necklace.

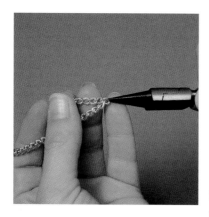

**7.**

Use pliers to break the chain into even lengths. Count how many links are required for each piece and snap open the link one beyond this.

**8.**

Use pliers to open a jump ring, slip the ring over the charm, and through the end link in the length of chain. Close securely. Repeat on the other side of the charm.

**9.**

Insert an eye pin through a crystal bead. Trim excess wire with cutters, leaving enough wire to turn a loop with pliers on the opposite end to the eye.

**10.**

Open up a jump ring, slip it through the free end of a length of chain, and through the loop on the crystal bead and close. Join the remaining loop on the bead to another length of chain in the same way. Join the last 2 charms to a necklace clasp instead of to the crystal bead.

**11.**

Glue jewel stones to the center of each flower to finish.

## Variations on a Theme

Hearts are another variation on the basic theme. To add a glamorous sparkle, they have been linked by a chain to larger crystals taken from a chandelier (right).

In this contemporary design, Fimo is rolled into tube beads and a large "nugget" to make a pendant drop. Paint the shapes gold or silver and link together with a matching chain (far right).

Diamonds & PEARLS

## Design Tips

Use vintage beads to produce an antique finish, especially for designs inspired by the past.

To make a larger tassel with more beaded strands, work each side of the necklace on three or four threads instead of two. Remember that tassels always look better with an odd number of strands.

Experiment by adding more beads to each single strand of thread. If you opt for more than two threads on each side, try beading all of them before bringing them back together through a single bead.

Twisting or braiding the divided strands can create spectacular effects.

Use the same basic techniques to create different effects with alternative bead styles. Try substituting bugle beads for the pearls, and glass rocailles for the crystals to give the necklace a more delicate finish.

THE DECADES OF THE 1920s AND 1930s, THE ERA of the flapper and of art deco design, produced truly creative jewelry design that is still very popular today. Style books on this period can be excellent sources of inspiration for your own individual designs. This 1930s-inspired necklace is worked in a sophisticated combination of pearls and rosettes of crystal beads, and finished with a central, elegant, beaded tassel that was all the rage at the time. The touch of sparkle from the light-reflecting crystals gives this particular bead combination the magic and formality perfect for evening wear. To transform this necklace for a more relaxed look, choose different colors, styles, and even bead sizes—try all wooden beads in contrasting colors, as in the wooden necklace in *Variations on a Theme*.

*Scissors, cotton thread, and fine needles*

# DIAMONDS & PEARLS

## Getting Started

Each side of this necklace comprises 2 pieces of thread, 44 inches / 112 cm long. The thread pair is divided, beaded individually, and then brought back together again to create the crystal rosettes. When each side is the length you want, take the threads of both through a large central bead and then bead each individual thread to form the tassel. Use an odd number of beaded strands for the tassels.

## You Will Need

2 calotte crimps
Pliers
Strong cotton thread
Small pearls and crystal beads
2 fine needles
1 diamanté rondelle
1 large crystal bead
Glue (optional)
Necklace clasp

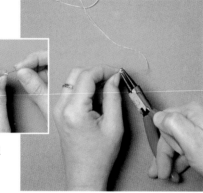

**1.** Cut 4 strands of thread to the length required for each side of the necklace (including the tassel) plus 12 inches / 31 cm. Knot the strands together in pairs and thread each pair through a calotte. With the knot sitting neatly in the cup of the calotte, use a pair of pliers to secure it firmly over the threads.

**2.** Working one side at a time, thread each length of cotton thread through a needle and then take both needles through 5 pearls and 1 crystal. Separate the threads and add 2 crystals to each. Bring the threads together again by taking both needles through a crystal. Pull the threads taut and push the beads back toward the calotte, making sure the crystals form an even shape.

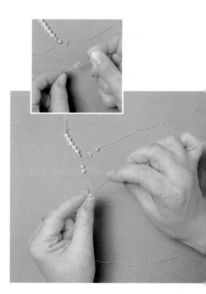

**3.**

Repeat steps 2 and 3 until each side is the right length to begin working the tassel, making sure both sides are identical. Take all four strands through the diamanté rondelle and then through the large crystal bead.

**4.**

Work 2 of the 4 threads together. Thread each with alternating pearl and crystal beads to the length required. Wrap the thread around the last bead, and take the needle back through the rest of the beads on the strand and the large crystal.

**5.**

When all the strands have been worked, knot the threads securely together between the crystal and the rondelle. Add a dab of glue to

secure the knot if required. To finish, slip the loop of each calotte through a loop on the necklace clasp and secure using pliers.

## Variations on a Theme

Wooden beads in contrasting colors give this necklace, which is worked on the entire length of 2 strands of thread, a more playful, less formal look than the diamonds and pearls project (right).

To complete the shimmering effect of this 3 strand necklace, a decorative filigree bell cap and hanger are added (far right).

# Marbled
## BEADS

Begin working with just two or three different colors until you've mastered the marbling techniques, then experiment with more extensive color combinations.

Include white to highlight the other colors, but beware—if the color combination is too subtle, all the colors will merge together.

No two beads will be exactly the same; if you have to make a second Fimo braid to get the required number of beads, these will be slightly different again.

Intersperse plain beads from each of the marbling colors with the decorative beads for a different finished effect.

Vary the shape of the beads. Try molding cylinders, ovals, or squares, and mix them all together for a more eclectic necklace design.

String heavy clay beads onto a strong thread like nylon or tiger tail.

THIS SOPHISTICATED MARBLED BEAD NECKLACE is made with synthetic modeling clays that are soft, malleable, and easy to mold into a variety of bead shapes. One of the big advantages these polymer clays have over traditional cold clays is that they set hard in low-temperature ovens and are so robust they won't shatter if dropped. A coat of varnish increases the depth of the colors and produces a finish similar to kiln-fired ceramic beads. The range of colors available is extensive— they can be used on their own or, with a little practice, blended together to create spectacular marbled effects. No two beads will be the same, but beads worked in the same color combinations will mix together beautifully to be made up into stunning necklaces. Once you have mastered the basic marbling techniques, the possibilities are endless.

*Fimo and scissors*

# MARBLED BEADS

## Getting Started

To make the beads for this necklace, knead the Fimo with your thumbs and fingers until really soft and pliable, to make it easier to roll and to prevent cracking or air bubbles. Always wash your hands when changing colors to prevent a color rubbing off on the other and spoiling the finished effect. Cut a length of nylon thread into 30 inches / 76 cm plus 3 inches / 8 cm for knotting.

## You Will Need

FOR THE BEADS
Fimo in 3 different colors
Craft knife
Toothpick
Varnish

❖

FOR THE NECKLACE
Nylon thread
2 calotte crimps
Sewing needle
Coordinating plain beads (optional)
Small silver spacer beads (optional)
Necklace clasp
Pliers

**1.**

Break off a piece of Fimo from each block and roll between the palms of your hands to form logs.

**2.**

Wrap the different colors around each other as if you were working a braid. Gently compress the braid in your hands, then roll all 3 colors together to form a log shape again. Fold the log in half, twist the halves together, and knead to blend the colors together.

**3.**

Continue twisting and kneading until you have the desired marbled effect, then roll out on a flat surface into a log with a diameter of approximately ½ inch / 1 cm.

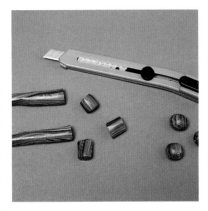

Cut small pieces from the log using a craft knife and roll into balls between the palms of your hands. Make as many beads as you need for the length of necklace required, rolling out more Fimo if needed.

## 5

Push a toothpick through each bead's center, remove carefully, and insert back through the hole from the other end. Reshape the beads (not closing the hole) and smooth rough edges. Bake in a low-temperature oven. Leave to cool and spray or paint with varnish.

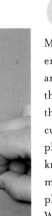

Make a large knot in one end of the nylon thread and pull the other through a calotte so that the knot sits in the cup of the calotte. Use pliers to close it over the knot. String on the marbled beads with plain and silver beads. When finished, take the end of thread through the hole in a calotte and, at the last bead, knot and close the calotte over the knot. Attach the necklace clasp to a loop on the calotte. Close with pliers.

## Variations on a Theme

To make this black and white beaded necklace, mold large beads from marbled Fimo and thread onto leather thong that is knotted on both sides of each bead to keep them in place (right).

The contrast between frosted and marbled beads makes this a particularly striking necklace (far right).

Sapphire & Silver
LINKS

Sketch your design on paper first or work it out by laying the beads on a flat surface.

Vary the lengths of the chain links to create a different effect, making sure that they are the same length on each side.

Practice making perfect loops in the top of a head pin using round-nosed pliers. It is important that the loops close securely over the chain links or the beads will fall off when worn.

If you are working with several colors or a mix of completely different beads, work the necklace from the center to get the balance right. Too many big beads or beads of the same color on one side, for example, will spoil the effect.

STRINGING BEADS ONTO THREAD IS NOT THE ONLY way of making necklaces; they can also be linked together using eye and head pins. Adding small lengths of chain between each bead or group of beads makes a stylish finishing touch. You can choose beads in varied hues of one color, like the project illustrated here, or use brilliant multicolored beads that look like candy. More delicate effects can be created by working with smaller beads and joining them together with bought metal links available from jewelry specialists. Or you can use plastic, glass, or ceramic beads; it is a great way to use up odd beads hidden at the bottom of your bead box or to rework a broken necklace. Once you are experienced at wiring and linking the beads together, you'll discover the endless design possibilities.

*Selection of beads*

# SAPPHIRE & SILVER LINKS

## Getting Started

For this long necklace, each bead is threaded onto an eye pin, which links the beads to each other and to short lengths of chain. Cut a piece of chain to approximately 36 inches / 91 cm and snip into segments about 1 ½ inches / 4 cm long.

Chain
A selection of beads
Eye pins
Wire cutters
Round-nosed pliers
2 jump rings
Necklace clasp

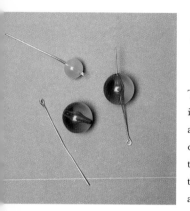

**1.**

To join groups of beads individually to one another, thread each onto an eye pin. If the pin slips straight through the hole, add a small stopper bead.

**2.**

Trim the wire to leave about ⅜ inch / 1 cm and, using the tips of a pair of round-nosed pliers, turn the wire into a neat loop.

**3.**

Open up the loops again with pliers to join to the loop on the next bead.

**4.**

To wire a single bead or block of several beads, thread them all onto an eye pin. Trim and turn a loop as before.

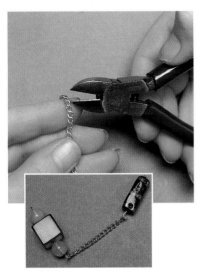

**5.** Break the chain into the lengths required, snipping the joint in the link one beyond the link you require. Open the loop on a single bead or bead group, and slip it through the end link on a length of chain. Close it securely using pliers.

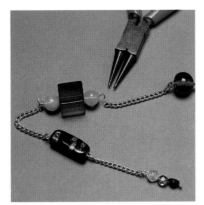

**6.** Continue linking the bead groups and chain together, keeping the design symmetrical, until you have a long necklace.

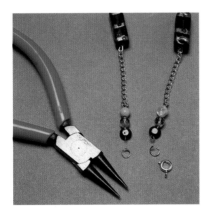

**7.** Join a jump ring to each end of the finished necklace and a necklace clasp to the other.

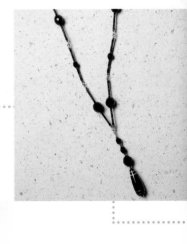

## Variations on a Theme

Beads in contrasting colors and sizes are mixed with small crystal to create an ethereal necklace (right).

An exotic hanging pendant distinguishes this elegant necklace of multifaceted black beads, tiny copper, black and gold beads, and thin black tubular beads (far right).

# Medium NECKLACES

Medium-length necklaces are easy for most people to wear and are perfect for adding just the right finishing touch to an outfit. You can make simple strings from a combination of interesting beads or, with a little inspiration, create more extravagant and unusual designs. Transform wrapping paper or handmade paper into glossy beads in minutes. Create festive necklaces from multicolored wooden beads cleverly linked by a simple length of chain. For a more international look, string a selection of antiqued silver charms in interesting shapes. Display a collection of beautiful shells for everyone to see by wearing them on a necklace interspersed with complementary beads. Combine fabric remnants with matching frosted beads to make a soft, pretty fabric puff necklace. To create a classic beaded necklace, use Fimo to make imitation millefiori, Venetian beads that offer a swirl of colors.

Create your own variations once you have mastered the techniques shown in the step-by-step projects. Make different style millefiori canes and use them to completely cover the base bead. Experiment with different color combinations and bead sizes to alter the look of the bold chain necklace. Bring in other objects from the seashore, like starfish, bits of glass, or driftwood, to give the shell necklace a truly natural look.

Handpainted Paper
BEADS

Spray or paint beads with a couple of coats of varnish to give them a more durable finish.

For totally unique beads, paint large sheets of paper with your own designs, experimenting with different paint effects, such as marbling, sponging, striping, and stippling.

To add a decorative touch, run a metallic pen along the edge of each paper strip before rolling up.

If you make your own paper, add interesting texture to the paper with the ends of colored thread, fabric bits, herbs, flowers, and grasses.

Recycle wrapping paper and colorful magazine pages for beads that cost next to nothing—if you don't like the finished effect, you can always paint them with acrylic paints or even nail polish.

YOU MIGHT REMEMBER TEARING STRIPS FROM magazines or catalogues to make paper bead necklaces when you were a child. Now you can make more sophisticated paper beads that even resemble pretty ceramic beads by choosing the right paper and using the right techniques. The skills to make these beads are easy to master, and once you've had a little practice you can have a wonderful time creating lots of different effects. Experiment with unusual papers as well as with traditional wrapping papers. Shiny foil designs, textured handmade papers, and even your own hand-painted plain paper can all be used to great effect. You can vary the shape of each bead by cutting paper strips to different lengths, widths, and shapes—the longer the strip, the fatter the bead, and the wider the strip, the longer the bead.

*Varnish, spacer beads, calotte crimps, jump rings, clasp, and nylon thread*

# HANDPAINTED PAPER BEADS

## Getting Started

These beads are made from painted paper cut into 2 different shapes, and then rolled and glued. Use 2 sheets of paper, about 16 x 18 inches / 41 x 46 cm in size. Cut nylon thread for the necklace into a length of 24 inches / 61 cm, with a little extra for knotting.

**1.**

Lay the sheet of paper out on a flat surface and paint on a stripe design. Leave to dry. Paint another sheet of paper in one of the colors used in the stripe design and use the tip of the brush to add texture. Leave to dry.

**2.**

Lay the striped paper face down with the stripes falling vertically. Mark one edge of the paper in 1-inch / 2.5 cm-intervals. On the opposite edge, mark ½ inch / 1 cm in, then mark 1-inch- / 2.5 cm-intervals. Connect the marks on opposite edges of the paper, forming long triangles. Lay the plain painted paper wrong side down on a flat surface and mark on the vertical edge intervals of ½ inch / 1 cm. Use a ruler to join the marks together in parallel lines.

## You Will Need

### FOR THE PAPER BEADS
2 large sheets of paper
Poster paints in several colors
Large paintbrush
Pencil
Long ruler
Scissors
Toothpick or wooden skewer
PVA glue
Spray or paint-on varnish

~

### FOR THE NECKLACE
Needle
Nylon thread
2 calotte crimps
Gold spacer beads
1 head pin
3 jump rings
Necklace clasp
Pliers

**3.**

Cut out the strips you need. Discard outside edge strips. Roll triangles around a toothpick, starting at the widest end. Keep the roll tight with the tapering edges in the center. Roll the straight strips around a toothpick to form cylinder-shaped beads.

**5.**

Make a large knot in one end of the thread and place inside a calotte crimp. Close the calotte using pliers. String the paper beads onto the thread, alternating with gold spacer beads. Add the pendant when you reach the center front point, and work the second side of the necklace to match the first. Add a clasp and jump ring to the loops on the calotte crimps at the ends.

**4.**

Before the end of the bead, dab a little glue on the wrong side, then continue rolling. Hold until secure and slide off the toothpick. To make the beads last longer and look glossy, spray or paint with varnish. Make a central pendant by threading a gold bead onto a head pin, followed by a paper bead and another gold bead. Turn a loop in the top of the pin using round-nosed pliers, trimming any excess wire.

## Variations on a Theme

Mix colorful wrapping paper beads with beads of a similar shape and coordinating color, and string into a necklace in any length you want (right).

Handmade papers that you can buy from arts and crafts shops or that you make yourself give the rolled beads an interesting texture (far right).

Mardi Gras
BAUBLES

Practice making perfect loops in the top of a head pin using round-nosed pliers. It is important that the loops close securely over the chain links or the beads will fall off when worn.

If the holes of the bead are too big and the eye pins slip through the holes, add a small rocaille to act as a stopper bead.

When working with lots of colors or a mix of completely different beads, it is still important to balance the necklace. Too many large beads or beads of the same color on one side will spoil the effect. Working the necklace from the center will help you get the balance right.

Reuse beads from any broken necklaces you have, and look for interesting beads at flea markets, antique markets, or rummage sales.

THIS UNUSUAL NECKLACE IS MADE BY WIRING LOTS of colorful wooden beads onto a chain with gold eye pins to create a bold, festive design that completely covers the chain. The beads are relatively inexpensive and therefore affordable in the abundant quantities needed to make the necklace striking. You can also use plastic or glass beads, or even make your own out of papier-mâché or Fimo. For a really eclectic mix of beads, collect and string the odd beads you have in your bead box. For more restrained designs, work with a single color, two-tone colors, or a selection of hues, such as pretty pastels on a silver chain. Mixing together different-sized beads creates yet another look. Once you become skilled at wiring and linking the bead drops to the chain, you'll discover there are endless possibilities.

*Multicolor beads, eye pins, jump rings, and necklace clasp*

# MARDI GRAS BAUBLES

## Getting Started

Cut a length of chain to about 24 inches / 61 cm. To determine
how many beads you need, decide whether you join the beads to every
link or to every other link, then count up the number of links that
you will use. (Ignore the first link at both ends—these will join to a clasp.)
Then choose the same number of eye pins.

## You Will Need

A length of chain
Multicolor beads
Eye pins
Wire cutters
Round-nosed pliers
4 jump rings
Necklace clasp

**1.**

Thread all but 4 beads
onto an eye pin. Add
a small stopper bead if
the pin slips straight
through the hole.
Trim the wire to leave
approximately ¼ inch
/ .5 cm for the loop.

**2.**

Use the tips of a pair of
round-nosed pliers to
turn the wire into a
neat loop. Thread each
of the remaining 4
beads onto an eye pin.

**3.**

Trim with wire
cutters leaving about
½ inch / 1 cm. Use
pliers to make a loop
and then work the
wire into a spiral.

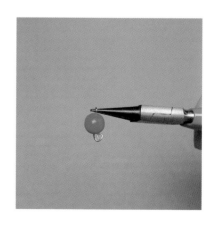

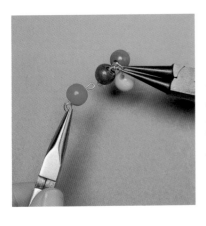

**4.** Open up a jump ring and thread through the eyes of the pins on the beads with spirals. Close the jump ring securely.

**5.** Open up a second jump ring and slip it through the first and the center front link on the chain. Close securely.

**6.** Open up the loops on the remaining beads and close again over a link in the chain, spacing them as needed.

**7.** Join a jump ring to one end of the chain and a necklace clasp and jump ring to the other.

## Variations on a Theme

Gold eye pins join ruby and clear crystals to a chain to create this stunning necklace (right).

These papier-mâché animal charms (far right) were shaped from plasticine before being covered with pasted strips of paper, like the beads in *Pretty Papier-Mâché*.

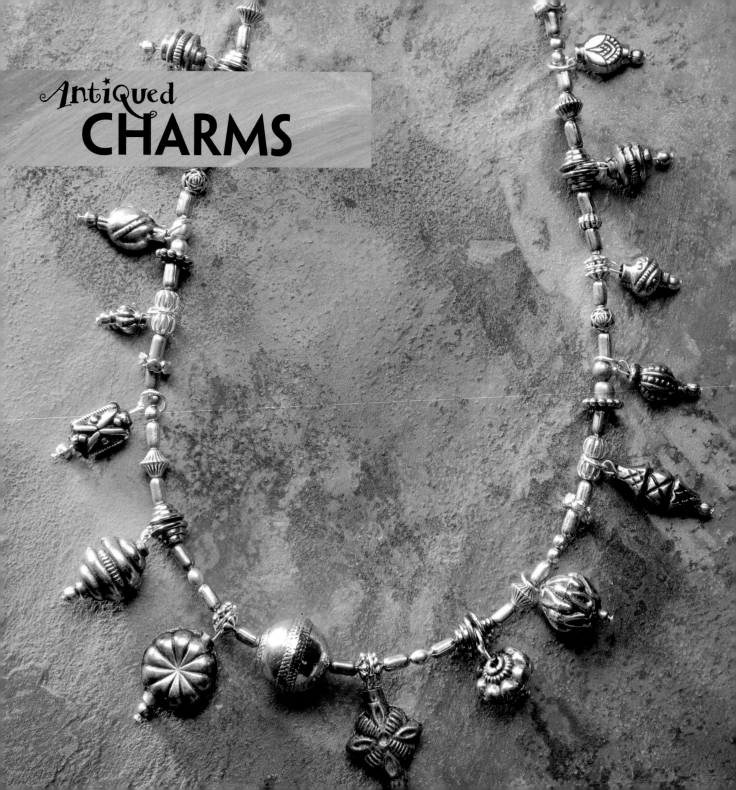

Antiqued
CHARMS

Before starting, sketch out your ideas on paper or lay the beads out on a flat surface to plan the design.

Practice making perfect loops in the top of a head pin using round-nosed pliers. It is important that the loops close securely or the charms will fall off when the necklace is worn.

If the holes of the charm are so big that the eye pins slip through them, add a small matching bead or rocaille to act as a stopper bead.

Work the necklace backward from the center to help with getting the balance right.

Always select an odd number of charms—one for the center and an even number for either side of the necklace.

T HIS STYLISH NECKLACE IS MADE FROM A selection of small silvery beads with a matte, almost antique finish that conjures up an international look. The decorative metal charms are hollow, so they are lightweight, and can be easily obtained from your bead supplier. As an alternative, you can use genuine silver charms that look a little tarnished. Or try shiny, highly polished, silvery beads to produce more of a refined effect. If you have collected them, use bits and pieces from broken earrings and necklaces in a similar color. Whatever charms you decide to wire, just make sure that they are similar in size. You won't need to make this necklace symmetrical (that is, position the same beads in the same place on both sides of the necklace)—just check that the overall design is visually balanced.

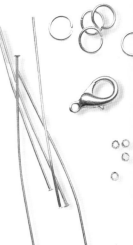

*Silvery beads, head pins, jump rings, necklace clasp, and crimp beads*

# ANTIQUED CHARMS

## Getting Started

For this design, it isn't important to use exactly the same kind and number of beads on each side of the necklace. Just thread on similar-sized beads, and place the charms at regular intervals, checking that the overall effect is balanced. Use tiger tail or nylon line that is approximately 24 inches / 61 cm long.

## You Will Need

Tiger tail or nylon line
2 crimp beads
Small silvery beads
11 to 15 hollow metal beads
Same number of head pins
Wire cutters
Round-nosed pliers
Needle-nosed pliers
11 to 15 jump rings
Small split ring
Necklace clasp

**1.**

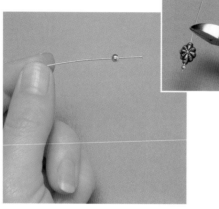

Thread a small metal bead onto a head pin. Add a metal charm and trim the wire leaving approximately ³⁄₈ inch / 1 cm.

**2.**

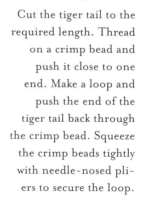

Use round-nosed pliers to turn a loop in the top of the wire.

**3.**

Cut the tiger tail to the required length. Thread on a crimp bead and push it close to one end. Make a loop and push the end of the tiger tail back through the crimp bead. Squeeze the crimp beads tightly with needle-nosed pliers to secure the loop.

**4.** Thread on beads, positioning them in matching pairs wherever you want to place a charm.

**5.** Slip a jump ring through the top of each charm and loop it over the tiger tail, between a pair of beads. Close to secure.

**6.** Thread on a crimp bead, make a loop in the tiger tail, and take the end back through the crimp. Squeeze tightly with pliers. Join a necklace clasp to the loop.

## Variations on a Theme

For a necklace that makes a bolder statement, use larger charms, like these gold and amber washers, spirals, and filigree shapes (right).

Slightly tarnished silver charms give this necklace a brilliant black onyx look (far right).

Always handle shells with care, as they can be quite delicate. To help make finer shells more durable, varnish or cover with several coats of clear-drying PVA glue.

Secure the shell on a piece of Blu Tak or plasticine when making holes, to keep them from moving around while you work.

Shells with a glossy luster or interesting markings look wonderful just as they are. Plain shells can be given a prettier look with a coat of varnish or metallic paint.

Mix the shells with complementary beads that will show them off to their best advantage but not overpower them.

Experiment by incorporating other objects from the seashore like small pieces of driftwood, starfish, and pretty pebbles.

Encase pebbles in a pretty wire cage with a loop at the top to connect to the necklace.

USING SHELLS TO MAKE SPECTACULAR NECKLACES like the one shown here is the perfect way to show off their exquisite shapes and varied colors. Looking for shells can become an addictive hobby especially when you realize the variety of ways they can be used in jewelry-making. Some are soft enough to take holes from a needle or bradawl, but for others you will need a hand drill and a fine bit to make the holes. Large shells make stunning pendants simply threaded onto thong, cord, or raffia. They also look sensational worn with pretty summer dresses. Smaller ones can be wired or linked with jump rings and joined to a bead necklace or natural raffia braid for more intricate designs. Look for specialty stores that sell huge varieties of shells including interesting slices like the ones used for this striking design.

*Needle, cotton thread, beads, and jeweler's wire*

# SENSATIONAL SEASHELLS

## Getting Started

Shell sections are wired and threaded into a necklace with complementary beads. Cut cotton thread into 2 lengths of 24 inches / 61 cm plus 6 inches / 15 cm for knotting. Begin threading the necklace with a length of beads before adding the first shell, so that none of the shells are hidden at the neck.

### You Will Need

Shells sliced into sections
Fine gold jeweler's wire
Wire cutters
Round-nosed pliers
Needle-nosed pliers
Strong cotton thread
2 calotte crimps
Needle
A selection of beads
Necklace clasp
Jump rings

**1.**

Slip the wire around the shell and cross it over close to the top. Use the pliers to wrap one end of the wire around itself as neatly as possible. Trim any excess with wire cutters.

**2.**

Make a small loop in the other end of the wire, close to the top of the shell; fold it over the point of round-nosed pliers and secure by wrapping the wire around itself again. Trim excess wire and use needle-nosed pliers to flatten sharp ends.

**3.**

Lay the shells out on a flat surface and decide on the order they are to be threaded.

**4.**

Cut the thread and make a large knot in one end. Place the knot in the "cup" of a calotte crimp and secure firmly with pliers.

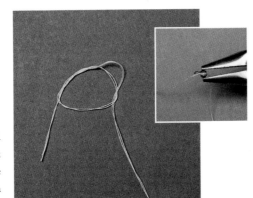

**5.**

Thread the lengths of cotton through a needle and make up the necklace. Work the necklace so it is symmetrical; begin with the beads before taking the thread through the loop of the first shell.

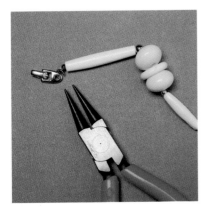

**6.**

Use pliers to open up a jump ring and slip through the loop on the necklace clasp and on the calotte. Close again to secure.

## Variations on a Theme

A string braid adds to the natural feel of this necklace (right) and provides the perfect base to wire beads and starfish. Paint the starfish with varnish to make them durable.

To hang these pretty shells from the bead necklace (far right), make tiny holes in the top of each piece of shell with a drill or needle, and thread onto the necklace.

Fun Fabric
BEADS

## Design Tips

Make a practice puff before starting on the necklace. Measure the drawn-up shape to determine how many puffs you will need to make the necklace the length you want.

Experiment with different shapes and decorations.

Choose fabrics to coordinate with a favorite outfit.

Look for special fabrics in remnant boxes.

Floppy fabrics can be stiffened with an iron-on interlining or coat of clear-drying PVA.

Add a nice finishing touch by mixing bought beads with fabric beads.

Make sure all edges are turned under to prevent fraying.

WHEN YOU CHOOSE TO INCLUDE FABRIC IN YOUR jewelry designs, you open up a whole new world of design ideas, fabric patterns, colors, and textures to choose from. If you know how to use a simple needle and thread, you can transform fabric remnants, scraps of embroidery thread, and leftover beads into wonderful jewelry. In this project, Suffolk Puffs (fabric pieces traditionally used in a kind of patchwork pattern) are strung together with frosted beads in pink hues to make a bright, fun necklace. You can also vary the design with pretty embroidery, worked by hand or on the sewing machine using metallic threads, to add stunning detail to simple tube beads. Look for unusual and glamorous fabric remnants like colorful silks, velvets, and lamés to turn into necklace masterpieces.

*Scraps of fabric and matching sewing thread*

# FUN FABRIC BEADS

## Getting Started

Use the clean lid of an old jelly jar, about 2 ½ inches / 6.5 cm in diameter, to trace circles in 2 scraps of fabric in different hues and patterns. Cut tiger tail to approximately 20 inches / 51 cm plus 6 inches / 15 cm for knotting. Find small beads for the center of each puff, larger beads for between each puff, and beads in contrasting shapes for each end of the necklace.

### You Will Need

Jelly jar lid
Marker pen
Scraps of fabric
Matching sewing thread
Sewing needle
Tiger tail
2 calotte crimps
Needle-nosed pliers
Various sizes of beads
Craft glue
Necklace clasp
Jump rings

**1.**

Draw circles 2 ½ inches / 6.5 cm in diameter on the wrong side of each piece of fabric. You will need an odd number of circles for the central pendant fabric, an even number for the other fabric.

**2.**

Cut out the circles carefully using small, sharp scissors.

**3.**

Turn the edges of each circle ¼ inch / .6 cm to the wrong side. Thread the needle and stitch evenly around the edges. Pull the thread up to gather the fabric and spread the gathers out evenly.

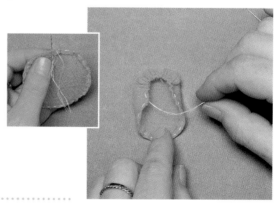

Oversew to secure the thread firmly on the wrong side. Make a knot in one end of the tiger tail and insert in the cup of a calotte crimp. Secure by squeezing the calotte together with pliers.

**5.**

Thread on the end beads, take the needle through the center of one side of a puff, bring it out through the center gap, and thread on a small bead. Take the needle back inside the puff and out at the center on the opposite side. Add a spacer bead and continue to the center.

**6.**

Take the needle through the top of the center motif so that it hangs down below the rest. Glue the bead in the center of the puff and leave to dry. Finish by joining a necklace clasp to a calotte and a jump ring to the other.

# Variations on a Theme

Exotic fabrics mixed with complementary ivory beads creates a bold necklace (right).

For a pretty, playful necklace, try using a floral and fruit-print fabric tied around beads with matching red thread (far right).

A book on the history of beads or even old pieces of jewelry can provide inspiration for millefiori designs.

Sketch designs on paper and color with felt-tip pens or paints that match the colors of the clays.

Cut out wedges of clay and substitute for or alternate with logs to get another style of design.

Experiment with base beads in different shapes—tubes, squares, cylinders, and ovals are all easy to mold in your hands.

Heavy clay beads need to be strung on a strong thread like nylon, but if you prefer to use a cotton or silk in a matching color use 4 to 6 strands together and knot the thread between each bead.

Use beads in brilliant contrasting colors or simple combinations like black and white.

MILLEFIORI BEADS WERE ORIGINALLY MADE FROM glass by the Venetians and were highly sought after all over the world. Translated, "Millefiori" means "a thousand flowers" because the Venetians could get so many slices of the same flower from one glass cane. Today, the same basic techniques can be applied to polymer clays to create spectacular beads like the ones shown here. Different colored clays in striking combinations are rolled and wrapped around each other to make the "millefiori cane." This is carefully and gently rolled to form a much narrower cane from which fine slices are cut and used to cover a plain base bead. The technique is not as difficult to master as it may seem and the cane can be used to make amazing jewelry on its own.

*Fimo and scissors*

# MAGNIFICENT MILLEFIORI

## Getting Started

Decorations for these beads are sliced from a tube or "cane" made of 7 logs of clay wrapped together. Knead the Fimo with your thumbs and fingers until really soft and pliable, to prevent cracks and to make it much easier to roll. Wash your hands when changing colors to prevent one hue rubbing off on another. Cut the nylon thread to a length of 24 inches / 61 cm plus 6 inches / 15 cm for knotting.

## You Will Need

### FOR THE MILLEFIORI CANE
Fimo in 4 different colors
Rolling pin
Craft knife

### FOR THE BASE BEADS
Fimo in other colors to go with the cane
Wooden skewer
Varnish

### FOR THE NECKLACE
Nylon thread
2 calotte crimps
Sewing needle
Small spacer beads
Necklace clasp
Pliers

**1.**

To make the center of the cane, use the palms of your hands to roll out a log from 1 color of Fimo approximately ¼ inch / 6 mm in diameter.

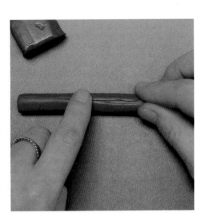

**2.**

From a block of Fimo in a contrasting color, roll out a sheet ⅛ inch / 3 mm thick and large enough to wrap over the log. Smooth the seam and then gently compress and roll the wrapped log between the palms of your hands.

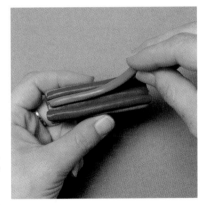

**3.**

Roll out 3 logs of equal diameter from each of the remaining colors, and build the cane by alternating the logs around the center, as shown. Gently compress together and roll between the palms of your hands.

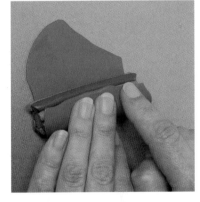

**4.**

Roll out another sheet of Fimo in one of the colors used for the center and wrap around the cane. Smooth the seam and gently compress together. You may find it easier to cut the cane into shorter lengths before wrapping with the last sheet of Fimo.

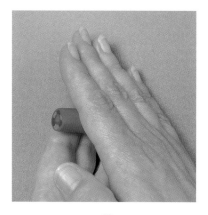

**5.** Roll the cane carefully and evenly between the palms of your hands first, then on a flat surface until the diameter is about ¼ inch / 6 mm.

**6.** To make base beads, roll them into balls or tubes. Cut off the misshapen end of the cane, then cut the rest into thin slices. Cover each bead with millefiori slices and roll gently in your palms to merge them together.

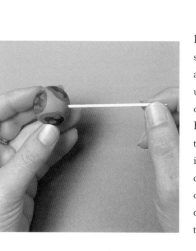

**7.** Leave the beads for several hours. Pierce a central hole in each using a wooden skewer or knitting needle. Bake in a low temperature oven, following instructions. Apply a coat of varnish to bring out all the colors. Let dry for 24 hours before threading the beads.

# Completing the Necklace

Cut the nylon thread to the length required, make a large knot in one end, and take the other end through a calotte. With the knot sitting neatly in the cup of the calotte, use pliers to secure the thread. String the beads on in the order you want, placing small spacer beads between each clay bead. Knot the remaining end of thread close to the last bead and secure to a calotte. Attach necklace clasp to loops on each calotte, closing the loops with pliers to secure.

# Variations on a Theme

Using 3 simple colors can also be very effective (right).

Make up a geometric design, like colorful squares, as a variation on the traditional flower-influenced canes (far right).

# Choker
# NECKLACES

Choker necklaces are glamorous and fun, and create a flattering frame for your face. Twist strands of glass rocaille beads to make a stunning choker necklace. Or transform ordinary metal washers from your hardware store into bold necklace beads by hand-painting them in a marbled finish. You can create spectacular retro necklaces using dramatic jet beads and sparkling diamanté. Use feathers or even pumpkin seeds to construct fabulous and unusual necklaces.

The choker necklaces that follow are very versatile; once you have mastered the step-by-step techniques supplied, you can develop variations on the design. Try interspersing larger beads randomly along the strands that make up the rope choker necklace. Experiment with colors and paint techniques to give the metal washers a totally different look. Or swap the jet beads for pearls to make a glamorous necklace for special evenings.

## Design Tips

It is essential to work in good light when stringing very small beads.

Delicate beads look best strung on a strong silk thread or invisible thread—anything heavier will spoil the effect.

Add the occasional large bead to a strand to give the necklace a different scale.

The more bead strands used to make up the choker, the more luxurious the finished look.

Instead of twisting the strands around each other, make them long enough to tie into a central knot.

For a central focus point, make a coordinating bead from Fimo or papier-mâché with a hole large enough to take all of the strands.

Look for and use unusual necklace clasps or recycled ones from broken necklaces.

TINY GLASS ROCAILLE BEADS ARE OFTEN USED in bead embroidery with bugle beads and sequins, but they also look fabulous strung into necklaces in a wide range of colors or worked in subtle color combinations to match a favorite outfit. For this rope choker, the beads are threaded onto fine silk threads that are then twisted around each other to create the rope style. Threading on all the beads for each strand takes a little patience but the finished design is worth the effort. The more strands you make, the more lavish the necklace will look. Twisting the strands together to form a "rope" is a classic jewelry design often worked in pearls, but there are many variations on this style. Experiment by twisting the strands in groups and then all together, and try loosely braiding groups of strands for another look.

*Rocaille beads and scissors*

# SHIMMERING MOONSTONES

## Getting Started

This necklace is made up of 4 groups of bead strands, with 3 bead strands in each group. Work 2 of these groups in the same color, and the other 2 in different, coordinating colors. Use a beading needle to thread several of the smaller beads onto the needle at once. Cut the thread into choker length, about 12 inches / 31 cm without the clasp, plus 1 inch / 2.5 cm to allow for twisting and another 12 inches / 31 cm for easy threading and knotting.

## You Will Need

Tiny glass beads in 3 different colors
Strong silk or invisible thread
Beading needle
8 calotte crimps
Pliers
4 jump rings
2 head pins
2 bell caps
Wire cutters
Necklace clasp

**1.**

Tie one end of a strand to a large stopper bead to prevent beads falling off while you work and thread on beads to the desired length. Tie the free end of the thread to a stopper bead and work another 2 strands to make up the group.

**2.**

Untie stopper beads and knot the 3 threads together. Slip the knot into a side-opening calotte, using pliers to close and secure the thread. At the other end, knot the threads together close to the last beads and secure with a calotte. Repeat for all strands.

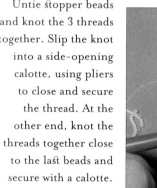

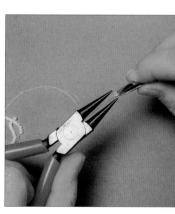

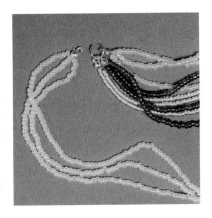

**3.**

Using pliers, open up a tiny jump ring, slip it through the loops of all the calottes at one end, and close to secure. Repeat for the opposite end.

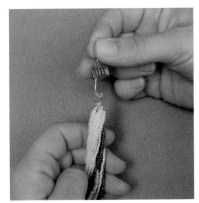

**4.**

Use pliers to turn a loop at one end of a head pin, slipping it through the jump ring before closing securely. Push the free end of the head pin through a bell cap hole. Pull it as far as it will go so that calottes and jump ring are covered. Trim the wire and turn another loop.

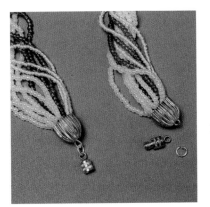

**5.**

Open up a jump ring and insert through the loop on the bell cap and through the loop on one part of the necklace clasp. Close securely using pliers.

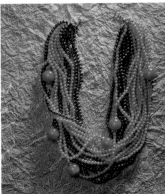

## Variations on a Theme

Larger glass beads have been used to make this stunning black and white necklace (right) and the five-hole filigree hanger adds a decorative finishing touch.

To create a really special necklace, use lots of bead strands together and add larger beads randomly along a few of the strands (far right).

**Fabulous FEATHERS**

Organize the feathers by size and lay out on a flat surface to work out your design.

Place larger or longer feathers toward the center to allow them to hang naturally and not interfere with your shoulder line.

If you think a feather is too long, carefully strip away as much as required from the base of the feather, not the top, or you will spoil the shape.

Look for unusual feathers—even ones from a colorful, unused feather duster.

To clean feathers you find outside, brush them gently with a toothbrush and sterilizing solution.

To create a tapered effect, choose longer, larger feathers for the center group and then matching pairs that gradually get shorter and finer on each side of the necklace.

FEATHERS ARE MORE FREQUENTLY ASSOCIATED WITH hat pins and Native American crafts than with necklaces, but they can be used to create unique, attractive necklace designs. Use smaller, finer feathers to produce more of a wispy look around your neck. A fishing tackle supplier is a great source for these kinds of feathers, as angling enthusiasts like to make their own colorful "flies" from feathers. Other feathers, such as ostrich and marabou, come in a fantastic range of colors; some specialists will even dye them to match a favorite fabric.

These larger feathers can be used to make striking pendants or central drops, or can be trimmed to use as charms in a necklace. Try interspersing metal spiral charms between the feathers to give the necklace more form and a little pizazz.

*Feathers and a length of chain*

# FABULOUS FEATHERS

## Getting Started

Organize the feathers into groups of gradually decreasing size. You will need enough jump rings to join each feather group and spiral charm, and to attach the necklace clasp. The jeweler's wire for the spirals should be in either gold or silver to match a choker length (about 12 inches / 31 cm) of chain.

## You Will Need

A selection of feathers
Square calotte crimps
All-purpose craft glue
Round-nosed pliers
Needle-nosed pliers
Pendant findings
Jeweler's wire
Wire cutters
A length of chain
Jump rings
Necklace clasp

### 1.

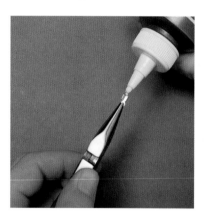

Add a blob of glue to the inside of a square calotte crimp.

### 2.

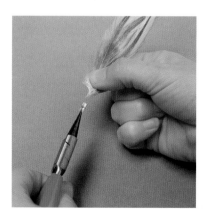

Insert the feathers into the calotte by size groups, positioning them so that from the front, they are splayed out to their best advantage.

### 3.

Use needle-nosed pliers to clamp each side of the calotte over the feathers. Leave to dry.

**4.** Insert both points of a pendant finding through the loop of the calotte on each group of feathers and squeeze together with your fingers or needle-nosed pliers to secure.

**5.** Cut a small length of wire approximately 2 inches / 5 cm long. Turn an initial loop in one end with round-nosed pliers and then continue to work the wire around itself to form a spiral the size needed. Trim the wire and form a loop at the free end by turning the wire over round-nosed pliers.

**6.** Work the necklace from the center point of the chain. To join the largest group of feathers to the center, open a jump ring with pliers, and insert it through both the top of the pendant loop and a link on the chain. Close.

Position the other groups at regular intervals from the center leaving room to link a metal spiral midway between each group. Join a necklace clasp to one end of the chain with a jump ring and attach a single jump ring to the other end.

## Variations on a Theme

Use the eye of a peacock feather (right) to make a stunning central charm, and position its spindly edges in small groups on either side.

A single black marabou feather trimmed with dramatic crystal and diamanté beads makes a striking pendant drop (far right).

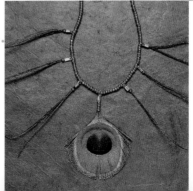

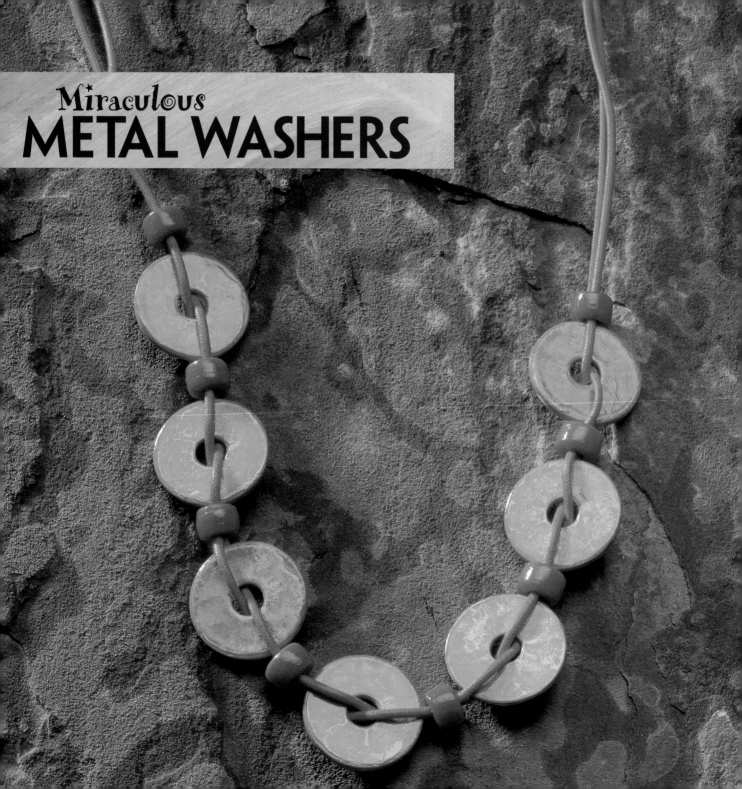

# Miraculous
# METAL WASHERS

First sketch out possible design ideas on paper and experiment with different paint effects.

Use artist's masking fluid, which can easily be rubbed off, to protect areas on the washer that you don't want to paint.

Paint a few practice washers to get the feel of how much paint to load onto your brush and to check the drying time—enamel paints stay tacky for a long time.

Link washers of different sizes together by starting with the smallest ones and working up to the largest at the center point.

Choose thong, cord, or ribbon in matching or contrasting colors and add matching beads between each washer.

MOST PEOPLE ARE AMAZED AT HOW THE MOST unlikely materials can be transformed into expensive-looking pieces of jewelry, but once you develop a jeweler's eye you will see the most mundane objects in a new light. The hardware store, for example, is a great source of unusual materials to transform into unique and stylish pieces of jewelry. This striking choker is made from ordinary metal washers that are painted orange and lemon to disguise their humble origin. The marbled paint effect is easy to achieve if you use hobby enamels, which come in a wide range of color combinations, from subtle to outrageous. Link the washers by weaving two strands of strong material—thong, cord, or even ribbon—through the washer center. Or hang them like charms from metal button backs.

*Hobby enamels, metal washers, paintbrush, and gesso*

# MIRACULOUS METAL WASHERS

## Getting Started

Choose an uneven number of washers for this necklace. Make sure that each washer is clean and free of dust or grease before you paint. Cut a piece of narrow leather thong into a length of 40 inches / 101 cm.

## You Will Need

Metal washers
Gesso
Paintbrush
Hobby enamels in 2 different colors
Narrow leather thong
Coordinating beads
Toothpicks

**1.**

Paint all the surfaces of the washer with gesso.

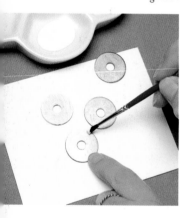

**2.**

Next add a coat of the highlight color. Check the paint instructions and leave for the recommended drying time before adding the next coat.

**4.**

Create the marbled effect by swirling the 2 colors together using a toothpick or similar object.

**3.**

Paint each washer again with the main color but do not leave it to dry. Working quickly, add blobs of the highlight color to the wet paint.

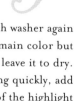

**5.**

Cut the thong in half and insert a length through the center hole of the first washer.

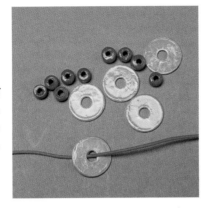

**6.**

Position the washer about 6 inches / 15 cm from one end and bring the other length of thong through the same hole but from the opposite direction.

**7.**

Push both ends of the thong through the center of a bead. Continue until all the washers have been threaded. Knot the thong close to the last washer on each side and make a knot in each end, or finish with a spring crimp or square calotte and a necklace clasp.

## Variations on a Theme

Combine ceramic paints in vibrant, contrasting colors to make a really wild choker (right). Add a textured finish by wrapping each washer in a piece of plastic while the paint is still tacky.

For a more glamorous look, glue tiny jewel stones to the washer surface and string them on a silver cord using groups of small washers between each bead (far right).

Jet & Diamanté
DRAMA

To avoid any pitfalls, work out more complex designs on paper before starting this necklace.

Measure your neck with a longer bead necklace or a string, following the curve of your neck.

Avoid making the necklace too short or it will look like it is strangling you.

Diamanté rondelles and spacers are quite expensive, so use them sparingly between groups of beads or substitute with tiny faceted crystal for a similar effect.

Scour antique markets, flea markets, and rummage sales for old clasps or necklaces that you can restring.

THE CLASSIC COMBINATION OF JET AND diamanté has existed in jewelry design for centuries. Real jet beads are expensive, but you can recreate the look with imitation replicas in glass or plastic. Faceted glass beads are the best choice; they are heavier and have a more realistic finish than their plastic equivalents. You can make a simple but striking necklace by just stringing the beads together with diamanté rondelles placed between each bead or bead group. More intricate designs, like the jet and diamanté necklace described here, have a greater impact especially when worked on several strands threaded through dramatic diamanté spacers. This design is also finished with an old clasp to give it the look of a genuine antique. Start a collection of unusual clasps to add a special finish to any of your designs.

*Cotton thread, black, faceted beads, diamanté rondelles, and spacer bars*

# JET & DIAMANTÉ DRAMA

## Getting Started

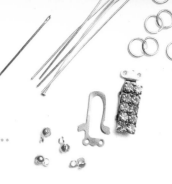

To make this 14 inch / 36 cm choker, cut black cotton thread into 4 strands of 20 inches / 51 cm each. Use the extra 6 inches / 15 cm for knotting and easy threading. The diamanté spacer bars have 3 holes: 2 holes for threading strands of double thread, and a third hole to join a jump ring and hanging beaded pin.

## You Will Need

Strong black cotton thread
4 calotte crimps
Round-nosed pliers
Needle-nosed pliers
Sewing needle
Small black, faceted beads
& diamanté rondelles
5 3-hole diamanté spacer bars
5 head pins
5 jump rings
Necklace clasp with 2 holes

**1.**

Knot the threads together in pairs. Secure each knot within a calotte crimp.

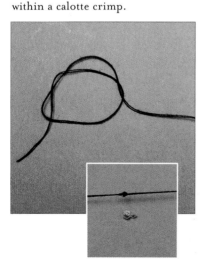

**2.**

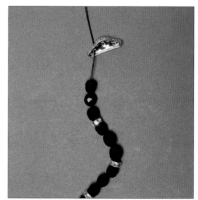

Thread a pair through a needle and string on the beads in the pattern required. For this design the black beads were strung in groups of 3, followed by a diamanté rondelle.

**3.**

Work the bead pattern to the start of the center design and replace the rondelle with a spacer bar, taking the needle through the top hole.

**4.**

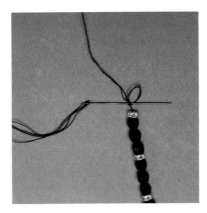

Add two beads and take the needle through the next spacer bar making sure it goes through the top hole again. Repeat until all the spacer bars are threaded on. Complete the string to match the first side. Use a needle to pull the knot close to the last bead.

**5.**

Work the second thread pair in the same way.

**6.**

Thread alternating beads and diamanté rondelles onto a head pin and turn a loop at the top of the pin with round-nosed pliers. Open up a jump ring and push it through both the bottom loop of a spacer bar and the loop on the beaded pin. Close to secure and attach the loop on each calotte to the holes on the necklace clasp, opening and closing them with pliers.

## Variations on a Theme

Larger beads and clear crystals (right) combine to create a more contemporary design.
Smaller black beads interspersed with small crystals produce a classic and delicate look (far right).

*Silvery*
**SEEDS**

Spray painting is the easiest way to color tiny seeds but if you have the time and the patience you will get a superior finish if you hand paint each seed.

Some spray varnishes and spray paints do not work together, so test them on a handful of seeds before continuing to make the necklace.

Spray the seeds in batches of the same color and string onto the thread in alternating colors or in groups of the same colors.

Use a fine needle and thread. Anything thicker will split the seeds (unless they have several coats of varnish).

To create a uniform look, insert the needle in the same place on each seed. For a varied effect, try moving the needle position each time.

Add beads between each seed to make them go further or for a striking look, string them all together.

THE SUPERMARKET SHELF CAN BE A SURPRISINGLY inspirational place to look for materials to make jewelry. With just a little creativity you can convert simple pasta shapes, lentils, or even dried seeds from melons or pumpkins into delightful necklace charms. They can be strung together on invisible thread or glued to cardboard to make motifs to hang as charms or as a central pendant. Or attach them to special pendant findings sprinkled on a chain, as in the ingenious gourd seed and chain necklace (See *Variations on a Theme*). This delicate seed necklace with its silver teeth and pretty central pendant is made from pumpkin seeds bought from a health store. The seeds are varnished to give them a more durable finish and coated with a metallic paint to imitate the look of expensive precious metals. You can also use other paint colors to match the necklace to a favorite outfit.

*Silver spray paint, invisible thread, and glass rocaille beads*

# SILVERY SEEDS

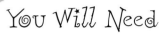

## Getting Started

Pumpkin seeds are spray-painted and then glued to a cardboard circle to make the central pendant for this necklace. The remaining seeds are pierced with a fine needle and strung along a piece of invisible thread 20 inches / 51 cm long (choker length plus an extra 6 inches / 15 cm for knotting and easy threading).

## You Will Need

Pumpkin seeds
Newspaper
Silver spray paint
Silver marker pen
Spray or paint-on varnish
Invisible thread
2 calotte crimps
Fine sewing needle
Small glass rocaille beads in several hues
Cardboard
Craft glue
Pendant finding
Necklace clasp
Jump rings
Pliers

## 1.

Scatter the seeds over a sheet of newspaper and spray the paint following instructions on the can—it is important to work in a well-ventilated area, preferably outside. Leave to dry and then turn the seeds over to spray the other side.

## 2.

Use a marker pen to touch up any areas the paint has missed, though the seeds also look attractive with some of the natural color showing through the paint.

## 3.

Cut out a small cardboard circle approximately ½ inch / 1 cm in diameter and paint it silver. Glue 4 seeds to the cardboard, forming a cross shape radiating from the center point. Leave to dry. Glue 4 more seeds to fill in the gaps as shown and leave to dry.

**4.**

Carefully pierce a hole at the top of 1 seed—not too close to the point or it will snap off—and open out the pendant finding, gently pushing the point through the holes as shown, squeezing it together between your fingers.

**5.**

Make a large knot in one end of the invisible thread and slip it into the "cup" of a calotte crimp. Press both sides of the crimp together using pliers. Thread the needle and work the necklace to the center point adding groups of rocailles between each seed. Pierce each seed in approximately the same position each time to get a uniform finished look.

**6.**

Slip a jump ring through the top loop of the pendant and thread onto the necklace. Work the second side of the necklace. Knot the thread close to the last group of rocailles and secure in a calotte crimp. Attach a necklace clasp to 1 calotte and jump ring to the other.

## Variations on a Theme

This striking necklace (right) has charms made from gourd seeds that were painted, varnished, and then fixed to pendant findings hung from a chain.

To create a totally different look, hang several striped sunflower seed charms from the necklace and intersperse them with black beads (far right).

# Acknowledgments

Grateful thanks to the many people without whose help and support this book would not have been published. First and most important, to my parents for their endless patience and for turning a blind eye when I used their home as a design studio. To Lindsey Stock and Jackie Schou for their additional design ideas, and to Paul Forrester for his creative photography. And, finally, to Shawna Mullen and Martha Wetherill, who made sense of everything I have written and gave valuable support and encouragement when times got tough.

# About the Author

Jo Moody is a journalist who has spent many years working for women's magazines that specialize in fashion and crafts. She is now a freelance stylist and writer, contributing features and designs to a variety of publications. Her childhood fascination with jewelry has developed into a passion—she loves rediscovering traditional crafts and using them in new ways to transform everyday things into truly beautiful jewelry.